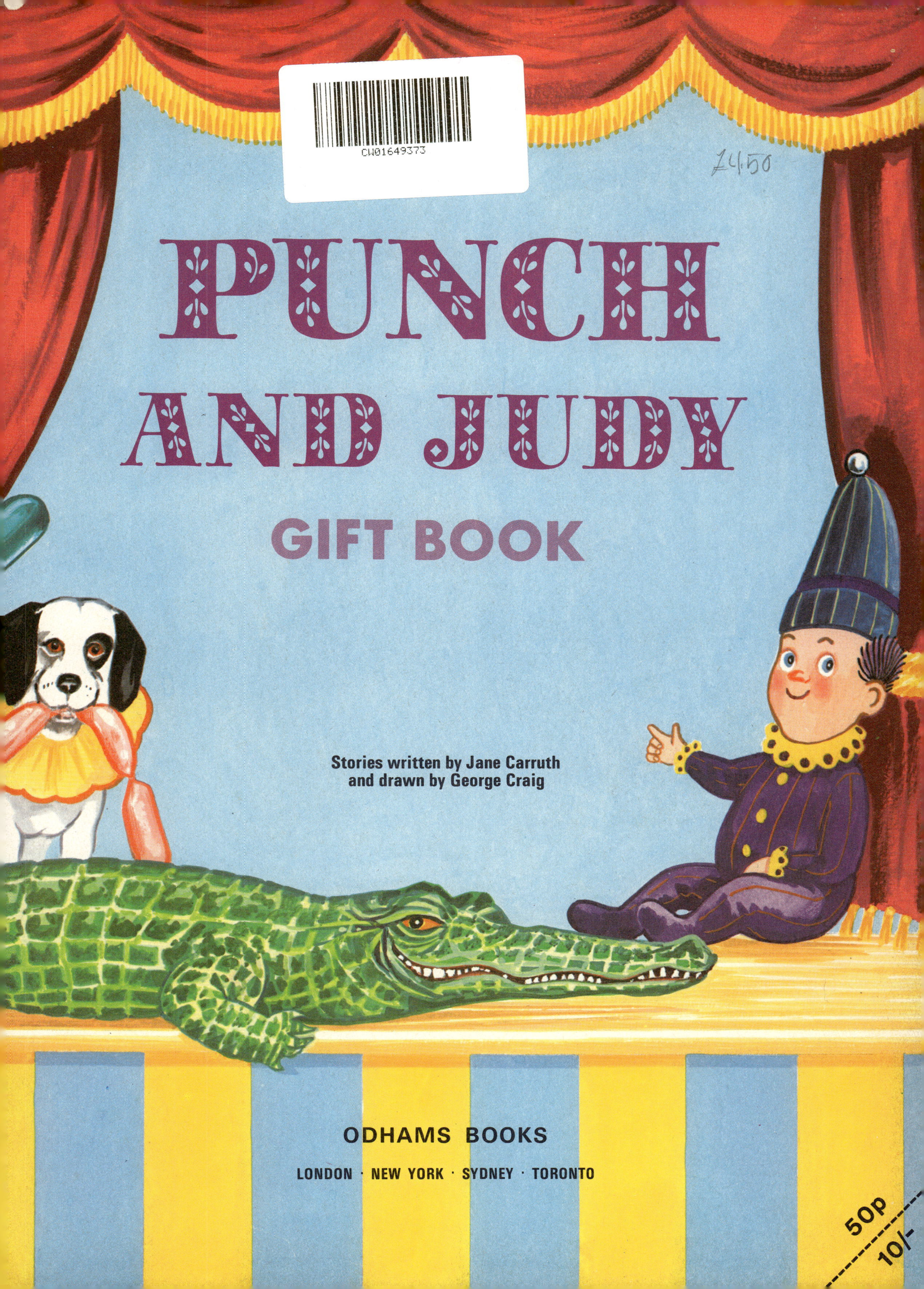

PUNCH AND JUDY

GIFT BOOK

Stories written by Jane Carruth
and drawn by George Craig

ODHAMS BOOKS

LONDON · NEW YORK · SYDNEY · TORONTO

Punch and Judy Take a Holiday

ONE DAY, Mr Punch said to his wife, Judy, "Judy, my love, I think it is time we had a holiday."

"You are quite right, husband," said Judy. "We have been giving two shows a day on the beach for a long time now. And I don't really think the sea air agrees with Baby."

Mr Punch and his wife were sitting by the window of their red and yellow caravan. This was their home, and they shared it with Baby, Toby the dog, the Crocodile, who lived in the bath, and the Clown. When the Clown and Toby were at home, the caravan seemed a little crowded. But today Joey, the Clown, had taken Toby for a walk, so Punch and Judy had the caravan to themselves – except, of course, for Baby who was asleep in the clothes basket, and the Crocodile in the bath.

"Where shall we go, my love?" asked Punch.

"I think Baby would like the smell of the countryside," said Judy.

"That's settled then," said Punch. "We'll tell the Policeman to tell the Clown that we have gone on holiday."

The Policeman lived next door in a blue and yellow caravan, and all Mr Punch had to do was to open his window and shout, "We're taking a holiday, Mr Policeman!"

When the Policeman heard this, he opened the door of his caravan and walked over to speak to Mr Punch. "I'll take care of everything," the Policeman said. "I'll tell Joey to give Toby his dog biscuits."

"And remind him about the Crocodile," said Judy. "Croc likes sprats for his supper."

"I'll do that," said the Policeman, who was always doing kind things for the Punch family – except, of course, when they were on the stage. Then the Policeman had to pretend to arrest Punch and put him in prison.

As soon as it was all settled, Judy said goodbye to the Crocodile, who was sleeping with one eye open. Then she told Mr Punch to take one side of Baby's basket by its rope handle while she took the other.

"We'll carry the basket between us," said Judy. On stage, Judy had to pretend to make Punch mad with her nagging. In real life she never nagged. She was so sweet and gentle that Punch treated her like a great lady.

The sun came out from behind a heavy black cloud as Punch and Judy set out down the road carrying Baby's basket between them.

When they came to a field of buttercups, Mr Punch was so excited that he nearly dropped his side of the basket. Baby opened his eyes and began to cry loudly, just as he did on the stage, and Judy picked him up and rocked him gently in her arms.

"We could sit in this field of buttercups and smell all the fresh country air," Punch cried, and he pushed open the gate.

"That's a very good idea," said Judy. "We can see if Baby likes butter!"

So they went into the field and sat down among the flowers. Baby stopped crying

when Judy lifted him out of the basket and put him among the buttercups. Then Mr Punch said he was hungry, so Judy brought out some sausages which she had wrapped up in paper and put in Baby's basket.

"These are not the *stage* sausages Toby steals," she laughed. "These are very tasty beef sausages."

"It is nice not to be working this afternoon," said Punch. "Do you think the children are missing us today?"

"I think they would be pleased to know we are having a holiday," said Judy. "And this fresh country air is very good for Baby . . ." she broke off. "Why, Punch, WHERE IS BABY? He was here a minute ago . . ."

"Don't worry," said Punch, jumping to his feet. "Baby must have crawled off while we were talking. He can't be far away."

Poor Judy's cheeks went quite pale, and her eyes filled with tears. "If anything has happened to Baby . . ." she began.

"How could it?" said Punch quickly. "We're sure to find him somewhere among all these buttercups."

Punch and Judy searched the field. They looked everywhere, even down rabbit holes, but there was no sign of Baby. He had completely vanished.

Judy began crying softly into a blue and white spotted handkerchief, and Mr Punch's long nose began to twitch, which was a sure sign that he was worried.

"We shall have to go back home and ask the Policeman to find Baby for us,"

Judy sobbed at last, sitting down beside a rabbit hole.

"But he won't know where to look," Punch answered. "There is only this field of buttercups. Baby couldn't open the field gate himself."

"I wish we had stayed at home," Judy whispered.

"Nonsense," Punch said. "Baby is here somewhere." And he sounded so cross that he made Judy think of Punch on the stage, when he had to pretend to throw Baby out of the window. "We'll go back to the basket, pack everything up and think things out properly . . ."

Just as they reached the basket, who should they see coming towards them but Joey the Clown, and with him was Toby.

"Hello, hello!" said Joey, beaming all over his face. "Toby wanted to run in the field, so we came here for our walk."

"We've lost Baby!" Judy cried. "Oh, I am glad to see you, Joey."

"Don't worry," said Joey, who was the happiest clown in the world. "Toby will find Baby . . . and look – he has already!" Everybody looked where Joey was pointing. There was Toby, wagging his tail and tugging at the blanket which Judy had used to keep Baby warm.

"Bless my long nose," said Punch, "Baby was in the basket all the time!"

"He must have crawled *under* the blanket and gone to sleep," said Judy, half crying and half laughing. "Clever Toby!"

Toby barked and began showing off while Judy kissed and hugged her baby. "I don't think I want any more holiday," Judy said at last. "Let's all go home, Punch. If we hurry, we can still give the children a Show before supper . . ."

Joey helped Punch to carry Baby in his basket, and Judy walked behind with Toby at her heels. When their caravan came in sight, there was the Policeman watching out for them.

"I am glad you didn't take a really *long* holiday, after all," the Policeman said, "for the children keep asking me when Punch and Judy are going to come."

"Well, we are here now," said Punch. "I'll just get my big stick and then we can start the Show."

The 5 Mistakes

Take your crayons and colour the picture below. See if you can discover the five mistakes our artist made when he drew his second picture in black and white.

ANSWERS:
Girl's scarf is shorter
Only two cords are tying back curtain
Punch's arm is lower
A bobble is missing from Punch's hat
Toby has lost a spot

Can You Find the Hidden Animals?

If you write the first letter of the objects in the boxes below the pictures, it will help you to find them.

1
2
3
4
5

ANSWERS: 1 Mouse 2 Sheep 3 Horse 4 Camel 5 Tiger

Crocodile's Toothache

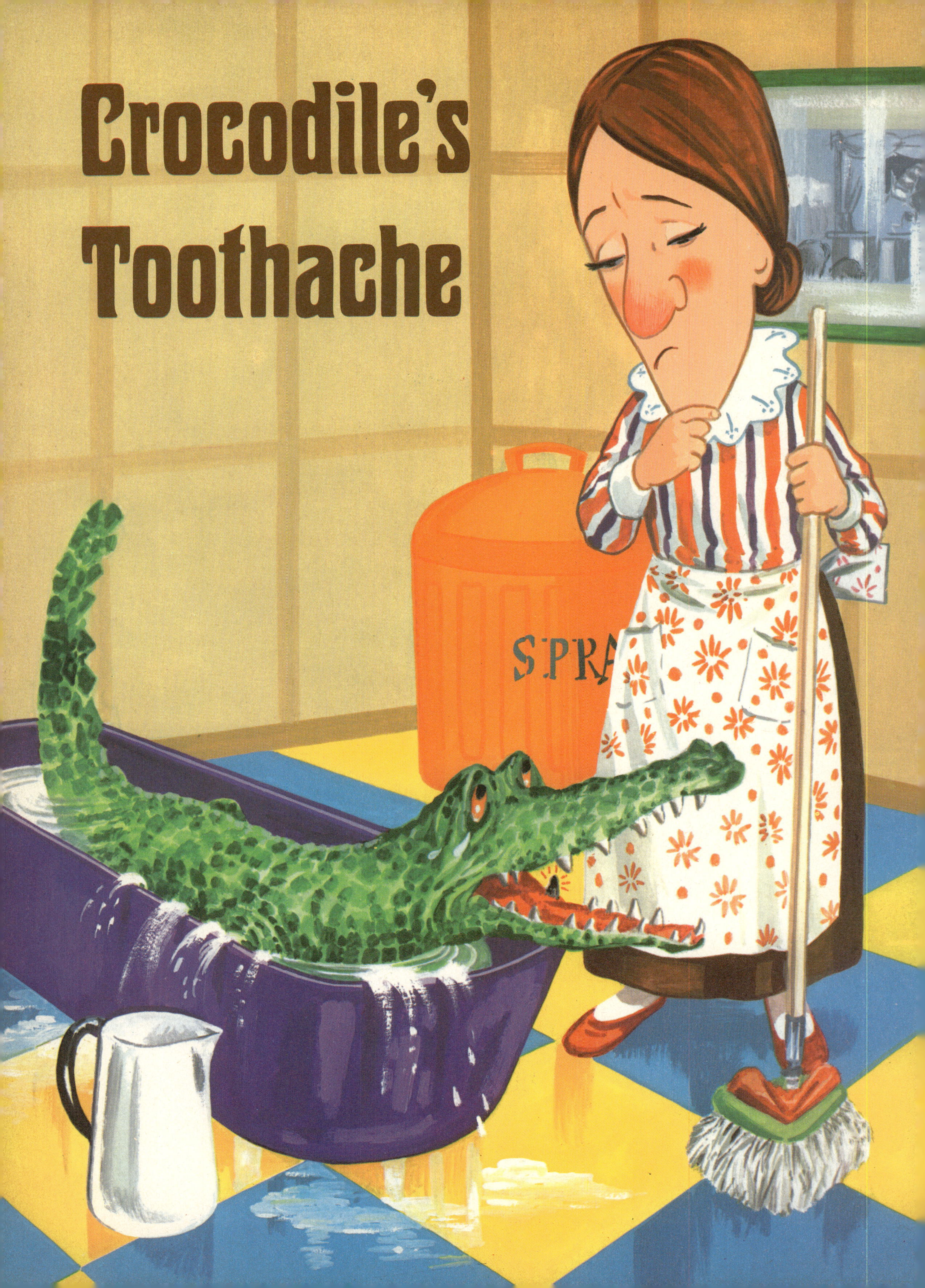

"I DON'T know what's the matter with Crocodile," Judy said to Punch, one morning. "He won't eat his breakfast today."

"Perhaps he's saving up for his Christmas dinner," said Punch. "You do fuss so about him."

"He looks miserable," said Judy, as she began clearing away the dishes. "And I don't know why . . ."

"Well, so long as he is all right for the Afternoon Performance," said Punch. "That's all I worry about . . ."

"Then you had better go and fetch the Doctor," said Judy.

"Very well," Punch replied. "I'm taking Toby to the park, so I'll be passing his place on the way."

As soon as Mr Punch and Toby had left the caravan, Judy went to look at the Crocodile again, lying in his bath.

"Tell Judy all about it," Judy said in her most motherly voice. "Have you got a tummy-ache, Crocodile?"

The Crocodile flipped his tail sideways, which was his way of saying "no".

"Then you must have a headache," said Judy.

But once again the Crocodile's tail flipped sideways.

Judy thought for a moment, then she cried, "I know! You've got a toothache. That's it, isn't it, Crocodile?"

This time, the Crocodile flipped his tail up and down once, and Judy knew that he was saying, "Yes, I have a toothache."

"You poor old Crocodile!" Judy exclaimed fondly. "Just open your mouth wide, and let me see if I can find that bad tooth!"

The Crocodile gave a big sigh and opened his mouth. Judy soon saw that one of his back teeth looked very black and nasty.

"That tooth will have to come out," Judy said. "So you'll have to be brave, Crocodile. Punch has gone for the Doctor, and he will help me pull it out for you." Then she patted the Crocodile's scaly head. "It won't hurt very much," she went on, "and when it is out, the fairies will come and take the bad tooth away and leave you a present."

At this, the Crocodile began to smile, and Judy went to see if the Doctor was anywhere in sight. Presently, she spotted him from the window. He was wobbling along on his bicycle, his black bag strapped on behind.

"Oh, Doctor," Judy exclaimed, as she ushered him into the neat little caravan, "I'm so glad you have come. I know what's the matter with Crocodile. He has toothache."

"Then it's the Dentist you want, *not* the Doctor," the Doctor said irritably. "It's a waste of my time to be here."

"I don't agree," said Judy. "You will be just as good as the Dentist. We only have to pull the bad tooth out. And you can help me . . ."

The Doctor hesitated, but Judy's

friendly smile won him over. "Very well," he said grumpily. "I'll help . . ."

The Crocodile was looking more miserable than ever when Judy and the Doctor bent over him. "H'mm," said the Doctor when he saw how big and strong the Crocodile's teeth were. "Pliers won't do; besides, I haven't got any. We'll put some strong string round that bad tooth – and pull."

"That's the very thing I thought of doing!" Judy cried. "And I have some string left over from tying up the Christmas parcels. It's very strong . . ."

The Crocodile kept quite quiet as Judy fixed the string round his bad tooth. When this was done, the Doctor said, "I'll count up to four. Then we'll both pull together."

"One, two, three, four, PULL!" shouted the Doctor.

But no matter how hard the Doctor and Judy pulled, the tooth would *not* come out.

"Dear me!" Judy panted at last. "It must be a very nasty tooth to want to stay in poor Crocodile's mouth and give him such pain. What shall we do now, Doctor?"

"I really don't know," replied the Doctor, scratching his head. "We can only try again, I suppose."

"Let's tell Crocodile to pull *against* us – like a tug-of-war," Judy suggested. And the Crocodile, whose ears were very sharp, flipped his scaly tail up and down twice to show that he understood without being told!

So, this time, the Crocodile jerked his head sharply when Judy and the Doctor began to tug. Out came the tooth, and down went the Doctor with Judy on top of him!

"Look, Doctor!" said Judy, after she had picked herself up. "Crocodile is smiling. He looks happy now. He can't be in pain any more – isn't that good?"

"I can't say *I* feel very good," the Doctor answered sourly. And with that, he brushed down his smart black coat and left the caravan.

Just as Judy was making a late breakfast

for the Crocodile, Mr Punch came home.

"Crocodile will be perfectly well for the Afternoon Performance," Judy told her husband. "It was only a bad tooth. He was very good and brave, and I told him the fairies would give him a present in exchange for his tooth. He wouldn't let me take it away."

"Then you had better see to it," said Punch, "for if I know Crocodile, he will keep that tooth for ever – unless he gets a present for it . . ."

"But we haven't any money to buy more presents," said Judy, in a worried voice. "We have used all our money for Christmas presents. And we can't give Crocodile his Christmas present *before* Christmas, can we?"

"Certainly not," said Punch.

"Well then," said Judy. "You'll have to think of something. And if you can't perhaps Joey will when he comes in for his elevenses."

Judy took the Crocodile a big dish of sprats. When she returned, she looked so upset that Punch thought the Crocodile must be ill again.

"No, it's not that," said Judy. "It's just that Crocodile says he is going to sleep after his breakfast so that the fairies will get the chance of taking his bad tooth away and leaving their present."

Soon loud snores could be heard coming from the direction of the bath, and Judy whispered, "That's Crocodile! He's fast asleep already . . . oh, and here's Joey at last!"

Joey the Clown came bouncing into the caravan; he kissed Judy, and then sat down at the table. "There hasn't been time to make any cocoa," Judy explained. "We're both terribly worried . . ." Then she told Joey about the Crocodile.

"I'm afraid I've spent all my money, too," said Joey. "The only thing I have that's really new is the woolly ski-cap Punch – er – gave me for my – er – birthday. It's – er – too tickly, Punch. I'm sorry. I – er – never liked to tell you."

"But it won't tickle Crocodile," Judy cried. "I mean – not with all his scales and everything . . ."

"Then you're very welcome to it," said Joey. And he went to his large box in the corner and got it out.

"Crocodile will love this," Judy said with delight. "We'll call it his new sleeping cap. I'll just tip-toe over and put it on his head right away."

"Don't forget to remove the tooth at the same time," Punch called after her. Judy nodded.

When the Crocodile woke up, he found himself with a smart red and white striped cap on his head. He was so pleased with it that he wouldn't let Judy take it off – not even for the Afternoon Performance.

And that was not the end of it – the very next morning the Crocodile pretended to have another toothache! But Judy guessed, by his smile, that he was only trying to get more presents from the fairies!

Punch and the Sausages
I'll show Judy how well I can cook these lovely sausages.
Hello, Punch! Don't forget to prick the sausages before you cut them.
Here you are. Prick the sausages with this fork.
Just as you say, Judy.
And when you've fried the sausages, see that I have the four fattest ones!
Very well, Judy, you can leave the sausages to me...

SALT
PEPPER
A pinch of salt and a dash of pepper... Judy will soon see what a splendid cook I am.
Toby, how dare you steal the sausages!
Let go of my sausages, you bad, bad dog!
Gr-rr! Gr-rr!
Ah-ha! Got you! Now, back to your kennel, Toby!
You can never do anything right, Punch!
It's all Toby's fault!

Ice-cream Man For a Day

I DO WISH the ice-cream man would come," Judy said to Punch one Saturday. "I really don't know what I shall do if he doesn't. It will spoil the little surprise birthday party I'm giving for Mr Policeman this afternoon."

"So it will," said Punch, who was busy pressing one of his stage costumes. "You can't have a party without ice-cream."

"That's what I say," said Judy, as she bustled about the caravan with her duster. "Oh dear, what should I do, Punch?"

Punch put down the iron. "Don't upset yourself, my love," he said. "I'll go out and look for him. I won't be long . . ."

"That's just like you, Punch," said Judy, giving her husband a loving smile. "And take Toby with you. That dog is always getting under my feet. A walk will quieten him down."

Toby barked and wagged his tail as Mr Punch called him, and soon they left the caravan. When they reached the road, Toby waited while Punch looked right, then left, then right again to give Toby practice in his road drill.

Then he said, "All clear, Toby!" And Toby trotted across to the other side of the road, where he waited for his master.

"We'll go to the park," Punch told Toby, as they walked along. "The ice-cream man might be at the gates."

But there was no sign of the ice-cream man at the park gates. Mr Punch scratched his nose and wondered where to look next.

"Woof woof!" Toby barked. "Take me for a walk in the park." So Punch went into the park and sat down on one of the small wooden seats to think.

He always had his best thoughts in the park, where the bushes were shaped like gnomes and witches and wizards, where the grass was always a brilliant green even in winter, and where the pond was as blue as the sky on a summer day. While Punch thought, Toby chased up and down until he was too tired to run any more.

"I know!" said Punch at last. "We'll try the Pleasure Palace. That's another place the ice-cream man visits."

So Mr Punch and Toby left the park and went to the Pleasure Palace.

Like the park, the Pleasure Palace was an unusual place. Here, there were

magic mirrors that made Punch look as round as a barrel and as tall as a giant; a tunnel of delights where he could meet Cinderella and Thumbelina and talk to Puss-in-Boots and the Three Little Pigs; a helter-skelter, and an animal roundabout that never stopped going round.

Mr Punch forgot about the ice-cream man as he whirled round and round on the roundabout, and then slid down the helter-skelter. When he *did* remember, he felt very ashamed, and he called sharply to Toby, who was looking at himself in one of the magic mirrors.

"Come on, we must leave here right away," said Punch. "We mustn't waste any more time. We'll go to the ice-cream man's house."

Mr Punch knew that the ice-cream man lived all by himself not far from the Pleasure Palace in a neat white cottage with a red roof and a green chimney. So, with Toby at his heels, he walked very fast until he got there. Then he knocked loudly on the door. Nothing happened.

"Dear me!" Punch said to himself. "The ice-cream man is not in the park and he isn't at the Pleasure Palace, and

now he isn't at home either. Where can he be?"

He was just going to walk away when suddenly he heard a shuffling and the sound of dragging feet. Then the door opened. And there, in person, was the ice-cream man!

"Who is it – atchoo – oh, it's you, Mr Punch. Atchoo! Atchoo! Oh, do go away, I have a d-dreadful – atchoo – c-cold . . ." the ice-cream man croaked in a hoarse whisper, before Punch could say a single word.

"So I see," said Punch. "And I am sorry, but I can't go away until I know what's going to happen about the ice-cream."

"All w-wasting – atchoo!" spluttered the poor ice-cream man. "Strawberry, vanilla and ch-chocolate – atchoo – all wasting . . ." And the ice-cream man hid his face in his big red and white spotted handkerchief so that he wouldn't sneeze any more cold germs over Mr Punch.

"So you've got the ice-cream all ready to sell!" exclaimed Punch.

"Of course – atchoo – I have," croaked the ice-cream man. "I c-collected it yesterday. This is today; today is when my c-cold came!"

"Then, I tell you what!" cried Punch, suddenly very excited. "Let me sell your ice-cream for you . . . most of the caravan folk will want some; and Judy needs lots for her party."

All the ice-cream man really wanted to do was to get back to his nice warm fire, so he said quickly, "Very well, Mr Punch. It's very k-kind of you – atchoo! It's all in the shed at the back of the cottage." And he reached up and took down a big key that lay on a shelf just inside the door. "Here is the key to the s-shed – atchoo!"

Mr Punch was delighted with himself.

He hurried round the back of the cottage, put the key in the shed door, and pushed it open. It was only then – at the sight of the tricycle and the big box over the front wheel – that he remembered how the ice-cream man went about his business of selling ice-cream.

"Goodness!" said Punch to himself. "I'll have to ride that thing . . ."

Now, although Mr Punch had been obliged to do many things both on and off the stage, he had never, never had to *ride* anything. And to begin with, he couldn't stop wobbling as he tried to steer the ice-cream tricycle in a straight line down the road. Nor did Toby help, for every now and then he would race round and round the tricycle, pretending he wanted Mr Punch to run him over.

When he got tired of this new game, Toby ran on ahead and waited for Mr Punch beside the first of the caravans.

Mr Punch sighed with relief when he too reached the caravans, and, feeling much braver, he pressed the musical horn which told everybody that the ice-cream man had arrived.

Its musical tune sounded very loudly in Punch's ears as he wobbled in and out among the caravans, but to his disappointment not a single caravan door opened, and not a single face appeared at any of the windows.

"That's very funny," said Punch. "It must be later than I thought. Perhaps they are all taking their afternoon nap."

Before he reached his own red and yellow caravan, Mr Punch saw the Policeman and the Clown talking together. "Hi!" he shouted, pressing his horn so hard that it stuck and went on sounding the same musical notes over and over again. "Any ice-creams today?"

"I'll have a strawberry ice-lolly, thank you," said Joey with a merry laugh.

"What about you, Mr Policeman?" asked Punch.

To his surprise, the Policeman pulled out his notebook.

"Now then," said the Policeman, in a voice Mr Punch had never heard him use before. "Have you got a licence?"

"A what?" asked Punch nervously.

"A licence," repeated the Policeman in the same stern voice. "A licence – that is a permit – to sell ice-cream . . ."

"Dear me, no," Punch said. "Do I need one?"

"You most certainly do," the Policeman said. He pulled out another small black book and thumbed through the pages until he found the one he wanted. "Rule 77: Highways & Byways: No vendor – that's you, Mr Punch – must sell any goods whatsoever without a licence."

Mr Punch's long nose began to twitch with anxiety. He grew so flustered that he took out a raspberry lolly instead of a strawberry one and almost threw it at Joey.

"Here, take it back," said the Clown. "I don't like raspberry flavour . . ." Then Joey looked at the Policeman, and began to smile. "Wait a minute," he said. "Mr Punch hasn't *sold* anybody anything yet . . ."

"Yes, he has," said the Policeman. "He has sold you an ice-lolly."

"No, he hasn't," said Joey. "I've just given it back."

Mr Punch looked anxiously from one face to the other, while Toby pranced and barked as if to say, "Oh, do hurry up and settle all this!"

"The law is the law," said the Police-man, beginning to write in his little notebook.

"And you sound just as if you were on

the stage and playing your usual stuffy part!" cried Punch, suddenly losing his temper. He got down from his tricycle and glared at the Policeman.

"Stop it – both of you!" exclaimed Joey, taking Mr Punch by the arm. "Why don't we all talk the whole thing over quietly? Let's ask Judy to make us a nice cup of tea."

Judy saw at once that something was wrong, but she soon settled them comfortably round the table, and somehow she kept Punch silent until the Policeman had drunk his cup of tea.

"Now, Punch," Judy said, "tell me all about it."

"It's all a big misunderstanding," said Punch, after he had explained about the ice-cream man.

"Of course it is," said the Clown.

"I can't see it that way myself," said the Policeman.

"Well, really!" Judy exclaimed. "I don't know what all the fuss is about. All Punch was doing was bringing me a load of ice-cream for SOMEBODY'S BIRTHDAY PARTY . . ." She looked straight at the Policeman. "Don't ask me whose birthday party . . ."

The Policeman coughed and stared into his cup. Then he sighed and put his notebook away. "I – I thought you had forgotten," he said. "And, well, that made me so unhappy that I wanted to arrest somebody . . . I never have, you know, except on the stage. And you did break Rule 77, Mr Punch . . ."

"He didn't," said the Clown. "Even if he meant to, he didn't."

"Now, about this – er – birthday party, Mr Policeman," said Judy quickly. "Why don't you send yourself off duty for the rest of the day, and get ready for it?"

And that is just what the Policeman did, and thanks to Mr Punch and all the ice-cream, the lollies, the sundaes and the cornets, he had the best birthday party of his whole life!

The Missing Crackers

Judy has hidden ten crackers. Can you help the Policeman and his friends to find them?

Toby's Adventure

ONE MORNING Judy actually lost her temper, and it was all Toby's fault.

Toby began the day by upsetting his full drinking bowl of water all over Judy's clean floor. Then he chewed up one of Mr Punch's slippers.

Judy was trying to mend the slipper before Mr Punch came home, when she heard a loud crash. Toby was back in the kitchen. He had jumped up on the table and knocked over a bowl of custard.

Poor Judy was nearly in tears when she saw the mess.

"Toby, you bad, bad dog!" she screamed. "I won't have you in the caravan a minute longer. Out you go!"

Toby was surprised to find himself outside. Usually, he was never allowed out unless Mr Punch was with him. He gave a pleased bark, pricked up his ears, and trotted away.

He knew exactly where he was going – to the park. This was his favourite place. But when he reached the park gates, the Policeman was already there.

"Hi, Toby!" the Policeman shouted. "You can't go into the park without your master. It's against the law." So saying, the Policeman ran towards Toby, waving his baton.

With an excited bark, Toby dived between the Policeman's legs, and scampered into the park. The Policeman scowled fiercely, and gave chase.

This was just what Toby wanted. He hid behind bushes, peeped out from behind trees, and ran under wooden benches. The Policeman was no match for Toby, and at last, puffing and blowing, he had to give up.

"Mr Punch will hear of this," he panted. "I'll go and fetch him at once." And with that he turned round and went away.

Toby was sorry to see the Policeman go – until he remembered the duck pond. "I'll have a game with the ducks now," Toby decided.

But the ducks were not a bit pleased to see him. They fluffed their feathers and quacked loudly and crossly as soon as Toby put a paw in their water.

"The same to you!" Toby barked, showing his fine white teeth. "You're just a lot of silly birds."

Toby was just thinking about chasing the ducks out of their own pond, when suddenly he heard a sobbing sound. He cocked his head on one side and listened. Then he trotted over to a clump of bushes.

There, to his surprise, he saw a golden-haired little girl. She was sitting on a comic, and drowning a big teddy bear with her tears.

Toby knew her at once. She was Mandy, the Showman's small daughter. He had often seen her watching the Punch and Judy Shows.

When Mandy saw Toby, she felt much better. She stopped crying and whispered, "Oh, Toby. Please take me home, Toby. Teddy and me are lost . . ."

Toby understood at once that Mandy wasn't playing a game, and that she really was lost. So he barked to tell her he understood. Then he tugged at Mandy's bright red cape, and she scrambled to her feet.

As they made their way to the park gates, Mandy told Toby how she had planned to show her new teddy bear the ducks. They had walked round and round the pond until they had seen all the ducks, and she had forgotten where the park gates were.

"I was very, very frightened . . ." she said, "but I'm not frightened now you're with me, Toby."

Toby held his tail higher than ever as he led the way forward, and he felt very important.

Meanwhile, the Policeman and Mr Punch were deep in conversation at the park gates.

"Well, if you'll take care of that bad dog of yours," the Policeman was saying,

"I'll take a look round for that naughty little Mandy."

"Indeed, I will," said Punch. "I'll give him a very sound talking to, when I do catch him."

"And I'll have to go without my nice hot dinner," said the Policeman glumly, "that is until I find Mandy."

Mr Punch suddenly coughed and pointed. "I – er – don't think you will, Mr Policeman," he said. "Just look who is coming along the path."

"Well I never!" exclaimed the Policeman. "If it isn't that dog of yours and little Mandy."

Toby gave a loud bark when he saw his master, and Mr Punch tried not to look too pleased or proud.

Then Mandy said, "Toby found me; I was frightened and lost. Isn't he clever?"

"I suppose he is," said the Policeman. "Now then, I'll take you home, Mandy."

"And I'll take *you* home, Toby," said Punch.

And that afternoon Toby had a wonderful surprise. A parcel arrived at Punch and Judy's caravan with Toby's name written all over it. Inside there was a pound of the best steak, and on a card were the words, *To Toby, with love from Mandy*.

Doggy Mix-up

These dogs have lost their heads. Can you help them to find the right ones?

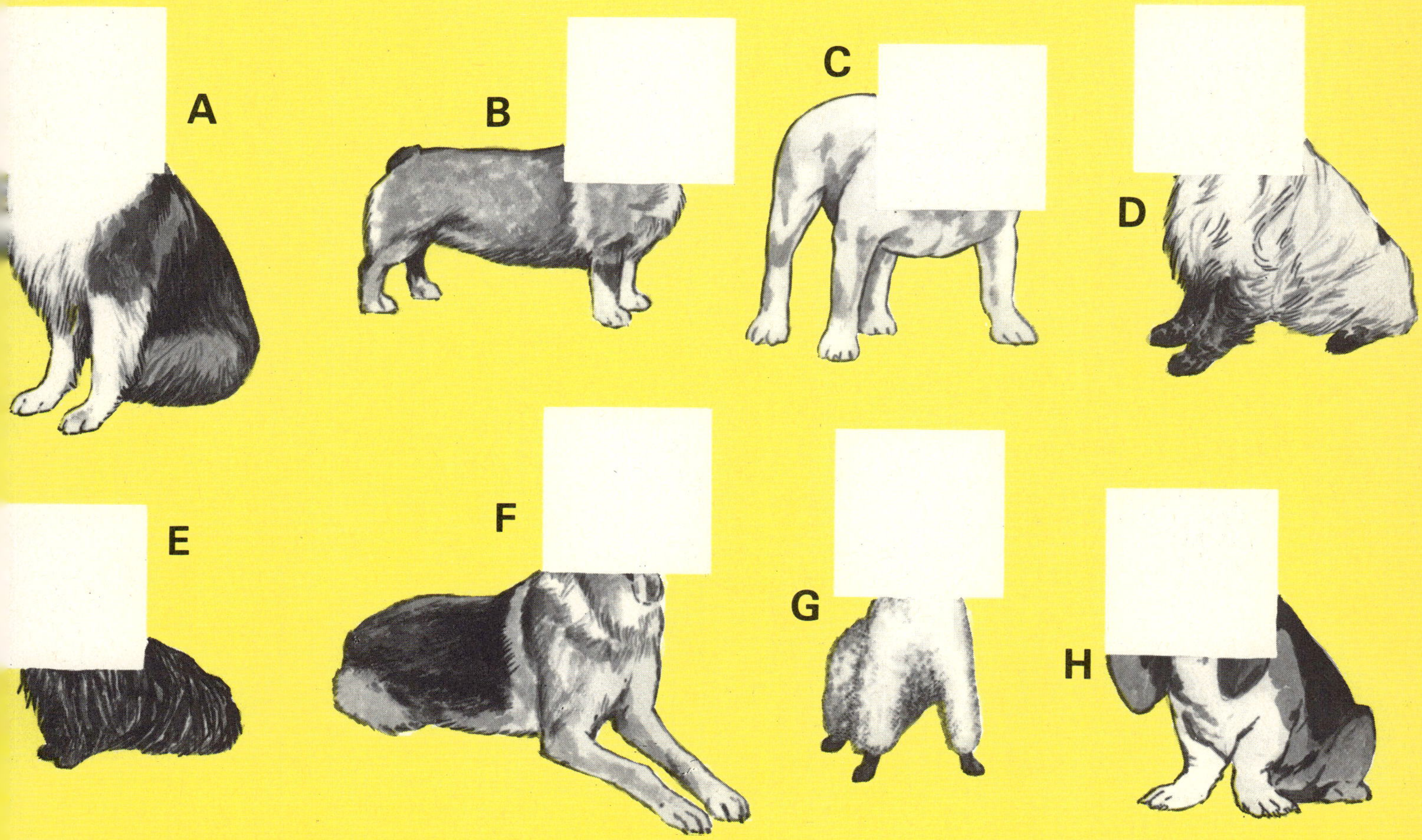

ANSWERS: A3. B7. C5. D2. E6. F4. G8. H1.

NO SUPPER FOR PUNCH!
Oh, do go to sleep, Baby. If you don't be quiet, I'll throw you out of the window!
Punch, how dare you say such a thing! My poor, poor Baby! Here, give him to me.
Hello, hello, hello! What's going on here then?
Punch is going to throw Baby out of the window...
I can't stand Baby's screams any longer.

You can't go round doing that sort of thing, Mr Punch. I arrest you in the name of the law.
Oh no you don't. Here, Judy, catch!
To your feet, Mr Punch. You are under arrest.
I'm not moving from this spot— and besides, my supper is ready.
The law is the law, Mr Punch. I'm taking you away.
Don't worry about your supper, Punch. I'll give it to Toby!

Judy's Christmas Present

MR PUNCH liked to buy his Christmas presents long before Christmas. And he always bought Judy's present first.

"I'm going to surprise Judy this year," he told his friend, the Policeman, when they met in the park. "I'm *not* going to give her anything *ordinary* this year, you know."

"Oh?" said the Policeman. "What are you going to give her, Mr Punch? Let me guess. A new pair of slippers."

"No," said Punch. "That's ordinary."

"I know," said the Policeman, "a new flowery apron."

"No," said Punch. "Try again."

The Policeman tipped his helmet to one side and thought hard. Then he exclaimed, "I've got it! You're going to give Judy a pearl necklace."

"No," said Punch. "Not a necklace. Nothing like that."

"Ear-rings, then," said the Policeman.

"No, no," Punch said, and then he added, "I told you it wasn't going to be an *ordinary* present. Slippers and aprons and pearl necklaces and ear-rings – these are all *ordinary* Christmas presents. My present is going to be *extraordinary* . . ."

"Then I give up," said the Policeman. "What is it?"

"I'll tell you," Punch said. "And, if you've got the time, you can come with me to buy it."

"I'd like that," said the Policeman. "I'm not expecting any crimes today, anyway. It's such a lovely sunny day. So what are you going to buy Judy?"

"It's – it's a *parrot*!" Punch cried. "Now, that's an *extraordinary* present, don't you think?"

"Indeed it is," said the Policeman. "I suppose you'll get your parrot from the Bird Man in the market."

"I'm on my way," Punch answered. "I just came into the park to give Toby a

he remarked, as they passed the Shoe Stall.

But Punch wouldn't even look.

When they came to the Apron Stall, the Policeman said, "And there's a flowery apron that would suit Judy down to the ground."

But Punch still wouldn't look. He wouldn't look when they came to the Jewellery Stall either, which sold pearl necklaces and ear-rings, and the Policeman stopped again. "A woman always likes a gift of jewellery," he said, as if he knew all about such things. This annoyed

run. Look, Toby's coming back now!"

The Policeman bent down and gave Toby a pat as the dog ran up to him. Then he straightened himself and his helmet, tightened his belt, and set off with Mr Punch for the Bird Man.

The Bird Man had his stall at the far end of the market, and as they walked along, the Policeman kept tugging at Mr Punch's arm.

"There's a nice pair of blue slippers,"

Mr Punch because he knew that the Policeman wasn't even married.

"I'm going to buy Judy a parrot," he said, at last. "And that's that!"

The Bird Man was just putting some seed into one of his canary cages when Mr Punch and the Policeman arrived at his stall.

"Good day," said Punch. "I want a parrot . . . a nice, big parrot with red and green feathers."

"Do you now, Mr Punch?" said the Bird Man, who was small and bent and spoke in a very high voice. "A parrot, you say . . . red and green feathers, you say . . . well, that might be difficult . . ."

Meanwhile, Mr Punch was looking about him. He saw yellow canaries, and blue and green budgerigars and a white cockatoo, but he had to admit he couldn't see a parrot – not one."

"You're a bird man," Punch said, rather shortly. "You should sell every kind of bird – and especially PARROTS!"

"Parrots are scarce this year," the Bird Man replied. "I couldn't interest you in a budgerigar, could I? Very nice pets they make. Very nice indeed."

"No," said Punch. "I want a parrot – and nothing but a parrot will do."

"I *did* have a parrot," said the Bird Man, when he saw that he couldn't change Punch's mind easily. "It was a fine parrot, too, with green and red feathers – very brilliant colouring."

"Then where is it?" Punch cried impatiently. "What did you do with it?"

"I sold it," said the Bird Man. "Sold it just one hour ago. And I won't be having

any more parrots in until after Christmas."

"What about slippers, then?" the Policeman whispered in Mr Punch's ear, but Punch shook his head angrily. "I want Judy to have a parrot for Christmas," he said. "And so she shall . . ."

"Look here, Bird Man," Punch went on, "if you tell me who bought your last parrot, they might be willing to sell it to me . . . at a profit, of course . . ."

"I can't do that," said the Bird Man.

Punch looked appealingly at the Policeman, and the Policeman said in his special stern voice, "I think you can, my good man, if the law requires you to . . ."

"Very well, then," said the Bird Man, "it was Mistress Judy!"

"What?" cried Punch. "Judy bought a parrot . . .?"

"For your Christmas present," said the Bird Man, giving a sly little cough. "It was to be an *extraordinary* present – something quite different."

"Well I never!" Punch exclaimed. And then he began to laugh. So did the Policeman. And so did the Bird Man.

Then Punch said to the Policeman, "What did you say about women liking jewellery? Perhaps you're right. Let's go and get one of those pearl necklaces before they are all sold."

Juggling Joey
Joey thinks he's the only one who can juggle... I'll show him that I can juggle too...
It takes years of practice to be a juggler. You'll never be a juggler, Punch, so don't get any ideas.
That's what you think. I'll soon show you! Give me those clubs!
Help! Where's that club gone?
What do you think you're doing, Punch? You're a public danger...
Ho-Ho! Now Punch is in trouble with Judy. It serves him right!

I told Punch he would never make a juggler. Now, Judy, I'll show you a bit of real juggling. Just hand me those plates...
They're my best china plates. What do you want with them?
Just watch me, everybody! I'm about to perform the most daring juggling act on this Earth...
Stop! Oh goodness!
Clever Joey! What a good juggler you are. It's just like being at the circus.
Now then, Toby. Just you go and give Joey a nice doggy kiss...
Help! Take that dog away! He's ruining my act.
Woof! Woof!
I'm seeing stars! It wasn't my fault... I'm the best juggler in the whole world, I tell you!
Ha-ha! You just try telling that to Judy. Something tells me she won't be interested!

The Parrots

Here are seven fine parrots, but only two are exactly the same. Do you know which ones are twins ?

ANSWER:

The twins are parrots A and G

CUSTARD PIE FOR TEA

ONE DAY when the circus was staying nearby, Joey asked Judy to take him to see it.

"Do you think that is wise?" Judy asked in a rather worried voice. "You know how you once longed to be a proper circus clown. If you go there, you might want to leave us for good and join the circus."

"Oh-ho!" laughed Joey. "I don't want to be a circus clown. What a joke! I like being a Punch and Judy clown better than anything in the whole world."

"Very well, then," said Judy. "Punch can stay at home and look after Baby, Toby and Crocodile. We'll go to the circus on our own."

Joey gave her a wide smile, and Judy put on her best bonnet – the one with the blue velvet ribbons – then she made a custard pie for Mr Punch's tea and put it in the oven.

"The pie will be all the better for my making it while wearing my best bonnet," she told Punch. "Now, take care of everything."

When they got to the circus, the only seats left were right in the front row, and soon Judy and Joey were comfortably settled.

Judy took a bag of jelly babies from her pocket, and Joey produced a packet of salt and vinegar crisps. Before long they were caught up in the excitement of

watching two big elephants waltzing round the ring.

Then came the sea lions, and Judy clapped loudly, for this was her favourite act. Once or twice she glanced at Joey, just in case he looked as if he were circus-sick! But his face was one big smile.

"It was silly of me to worry," Judy told herself, as she chewed a jelly baby. "Joey has forgotten all about wanting to be a circus clown."

After the sea lions came the dancing poodles, and with them Mocko, the clown. Mocko was a big, tall fellow with a fat, red nose and a funny checked hat with a long feather in it. Over his arm, he carried a bucket of water.

At the sight of Mocko, Joey began to clap. He clapped so loudly that Mocko looked at him. Then he came over to the ringside and called out, "Why, it's my friend, Joey! Come on, Joey, come into the ring and have some fun!"

Judy gasped. She tried to hold Joey back, but Joey was on his feet and pulling away from her. A moment later, he had leapt into the ring.

The audience laughed and cheered, for they thought Joey was part of the act. Mocko grinned and waved and then he tripped Joey up. Poor Joey rolled over and over, and the giant clown caught him by the ankles and swung him round and round.

The poodles began to yap madly; up and down the ring they raced, jumping through the hoops just when they wanted to.

"Stop it! Stop it!" Judy yelled. "Joey, come back to your seat. You're spoiling the act."

At last, the Ringmaster stepped into the ring. He looked very angry as he twirled his long black moustache.

He spoke sharply to the big clown, and

then turned to Joey. Joey dived between the Ringmaster's legs, and the Ringmaster, stepping quickly to one side, fell over the bucket of water.

Everyone in the audience, except Judy, laughed and cheered, but the Ringmaster's face was red with fury as he picked himself up.

Suddenly Mocko ran from the ring, and the dogs followed him. Joey then found himself alone with the Ringmaster, and he felt terribly scared. He ran to the side. The Ringmaster didn't try to catch him; instead, he nodded to the band, and the band began to play very loudly. Into the circus ring came the next act, the chimpanzees – and Joey was forgotten.

With a very sad face, Joey crept back to his seat.

"We're going home right away," Judy whispered fiercely. And she took Joey by the hand and led him out of the tent. "Whatever made you do it?" she went on, as they stood outside the Big Top.

"I don't really know, Judy," said Joey, hanging his head. "All I know is that I had to try being a circus clown."

"Well, did you like it?" Judy asked in a more kindly voice.

"Not really," said Joey. And he began to sneeze. "The sawdust went up my nose, and some of the water went down my neck. That big, tall clown was very rough, you know."

"There you are!" said Judy, with a sigh of relief. "We'll hurry home, and there will be custard pie for tea . . ."

"And muffins?" asked Joey, hopefully.

"Just for you," said Judy, and Joey knew he was forgiven.

Crocodile Fun
Oh dear, another sock to darn. Punch must eat the toes!
Did I hear you say something about eating? I could do with a bite myself.
That's *not* what I meant! I said you must eat your socks!
Now, now, don't talk to me like that!
Oh yes I shall!

Help! Help! I've been bitten!
Do something, Judy! Save me!
And to think I only came into the kitchen for a bite to eat!
Well, you've had a bite all right, Mr Punch– Crocodile's bite!
Just wait till I get hold of my stick again. I'll teach Crocodile a thing or two...
Oh no you won't. You'll clean up this mess. That's what you'll do, Punch!

A VISIT TO THE CIRCUS

For You To Paint

Happy Christmas – Birds!

"WHAT'S the matter, love?" Punch asked his wife. "You look quite miserable, and it's Christmas, too!"

Judy arranged her cap and fussed about with her apron. Then she said, "To tell you the truth, Punch, I'm thinking. Here we are – with everything we want for a jolly Christmas – and we haven't done a good deed yet between us!"

"But you're always kind," said Punch.

"That's not enough," said Judy.

"We're giving our friends a party," said Punch.

"That's not enough either," said Judy.

"Well, by my long nose, what is it?" Punch exclaimed at last, and he went over

to Baby's cradle and began to rock it.

"We haven't done a good Christmassy deed," Judy said. "We haven't done anything different . . ."

"I can't think what you mean," said Punch, and he stopped rocking the cradle. "I – I mean I can't think of anything. All our friends are in very good health . . ." He broke off as there was a sudden tap-tap on the window. "Oh, look, Judy, a robin – a little Christmas robin!" he exclaimed.

"Ah!" cried Judy triumphantly. "What about these poor little birds outside in all this snow?"

"Well, I don't think we have room for them in the caravan," Punch said, "even if they would come."

Judy was silent for a moment, then she said, "Punch, I've just thought. Supposing we make a little bird house – that would be a really good deed for Christmas . . ."

Poor Mr Punch! He was so looking forward to putting on his new warm slippers and eating hot chestnuts. But he couldn't bear to see Judy unhappy. So now he said at once, "If you want a bird house, Judy, you will have one."

"I'll help you," Judy said, and suddenly she was all smiles.

Mr Punch wound his cosy scarf round his neck and went outside to look for wood. Judy went into the kitchen, and began shredding suet and making up strings of peanuts for the birds to eat.

Mr Punch's fingers grew cold and numb as he began to make the bird table. And sometimes he hammered his thumb instead of the nail. But he couldn't give up – he couldn't let Judy down.

When he had finished making the bird table, it looked rather wobbly and lop-sided, but Judy said it was perfect.

"The only thing is, Punch," she said rather shyly, "you've made more of a table than a house. I – I thought of somewhere the poor little birds could shelter in."

Mr Punch scratched his head. Then he said, "I've got it! We'll fix Toby's old dog kennel on to the platform. It will be just right."

"How clever you are, Punch!" Judy cried happily.

Mr Punch worked very hard, and by the end of the morning, Toby's old kennel was securely fixed to the platform.

Then Judy came out with her coconut

shell, which she had filled with shredded suet; and a long string of peanuts.

Mr Punch filled a little plastic bowl with fresh water, and put some straw inside the kennel – though he wasn't quite sure if that was the right thing to do. "Anyway, Toby likes straw," he told himself, "and rabbits do . . ."

How quickly the morning passed!

"I don't know where the time has gone," said Punch, finally. "But I feel ready for my dinner with all that fresh air and exercise."

"So do I," Judy answered happily. "And I've tried to think of everything the birds would like for their Christmas dinner, too."

Then they both went inside. But, just before Judy served the turkey, Mr Punch had another idea. He fetched a piece of white cardboard. Then, with his box of paints, he painted on it the words: HAPPY CHRISTMAS – BIRDS! *from Punch and Judy*.

When he went outside again to fix the card on to the bird house, there, perched on the roof, was the Christmas robin.

"He knows, all right," Punch told Judy, as he sat down to his dinner. "I wouldn't be a bit surprised if we have some lovely bird carols this afternoon."

He was right, too, for the Christmas robin told all his friends about the bird house, and they came to see it for themselves.

And no one was more happy and contented that afternoon than Judy, as she listened to the birds outside enjoying their own special Christmas Day.

Toby